The

Columbo

Case Files

Season One

By Paul Hughes

The Columbo Case Files
Season One
By Paul Hughes

ISBN: 978-1-938039-09-6

P.O. Box 63
Orange, CA 92856

Contents

Introduction

Of essays, episodes, and evidence

This is the first in a series of books on *Columbo* — one for each season of the show and, I'd hope, some other efforts as we go. I want the books to help you enjoy the show more and more, which means I hope you already do.

I think the books will be fun for old desk sergeants and rookie beat cops alike. So whether you're the grizzled proprietor of Barney's Beanery or the new by-the-book partner, assigned to Columbo by the Captain, there's good stuff for all.

From his unending (and more than a little annoying) questions, to the trench coat and the car, to the dog and his signature 'closing' line — *Uh, just one more thing* … — it's all here.

The book comments on Lt. Columbo and his place in American culture ("The Columbo Essay") and the show itself ("Gee, That's Funny … "), along with a breakdown of episodes for the season (players, the story, best and worst scenes, and quotations) and a wrap-up ("Just One More Thing" — of course). We finish with the 'best' and 'worst' episodes for that season, and final thoughts.

I intend all this for a conversation on *Columbo*. You're welcome to continue that discussion with me (and many other fans) on Twitter. Try @PoetAndPriest (that's me) or @ColumboPhile (that's one of the most ardent Columbo fans on the Internet). We also have been known to use hashtags #Columbo and #ColumboTV.

> *Informative for newbies — why does he do that ...*
>
> *Interesting for old fans — debating the finer points ...*
>
> *And fun for both — as supplement to watching the shows ...*

Thank you for reading. If you have feedback (positive or negative), I'd appreciate, and enjoy it. Please leave comments or reviews in all the right places, and feel free to write me directly, too.

Enjoy!

Paul Hughes

The Columbo Essay

Why we watch, why it matters

For my wedding, I asked for and received the *Columbo* DVD collection. Complete to that point, it ended with the double helping of Seasons Six and Seven, and back copy text touting the guest stars like Kim Cattrall and Ed Begley, Jr. Plus a "captivating conclusion in these final episodes."

Those "final episodes" aired on TV in 1978. But instead of ending, *Columbo* kept coming for 25 more years. The last one ran in January 2003.

Altogether, the show aired over 32 years; 35 counting "Prescription: Murder," made in 1968. One half the biblical "three score and 10" is not, well, half-bad for TV.

And the Levinson & Link character is even older, dating to a mid-1960s play, and a single episode of a different TV show, with a different actor, in 1960. By then the man who would become iconic — Peter Falk as Lt. Columbo — had already been nominated twice for an Academy Award.

So the show began before I was born, the play is older than my parents' marriage, and even my dad, who introduced me to the 1970s TV series when I was in elementary school, hadn't himself graduated from high school by 1960.

Why then do I watch?

Why then do we?

*

When asked why they watch, most people say something about the character "Lt. Columbo." As so many of the episodes are quite similar to each other — through 35 years of episodes, we'll see recurring set-ups, returning guest stars (as murderer and/or victim, or even in supporting roles), and sets and backdrops used over and over — this makes sense. After all, if the shows are mainly the same, it's the character we're going to be interested in. And people care about people.

So even if it's the same Universal Studios backlot — where the show was made, and which often played its own role in episodes — and even as we attend a class on the social history of the 1970s, it's not exactly the same Lt. Columbo. The character develops.

So one thing we're saying is it's not just the character "Columbo" but the character *of* the man.

In fact, when Peter Falk himself was asked why the show endured, he always mentioned people connecting with "the lieutenant" and his homespun ways: his many stories of numberless quirky relatives, his affection for Mrs. Columbo, his never quite ready for prime time rumpled-ness ...

He was Everyman ... putting away murderers.

*

Of course, there have also been grievous mistakes in supposing why he's so popular.

For instance, in 1973, when the show was only two years old, a *New York Times* writer said "the most thoroughgoing satisfaction" of the show was "the assurance that those who dwell in marble and satin, those whose clothes, food, cars and mates are the very best *do not deserve it.*"

The emphasis is in the original. And it's not true.

That's not why we're satisfied and not why we connect with *Columbo* the show or Columbo the man. The point is *not* they don't deserve it. If we thought that, we'd be judging the killers based on their wealth — supposedly something *they* do to *us.*

No.

The point is *even the rich* are subject to the same laws, moral or otherwise, as we are. This isn't to say the rich don't get away with it in real life; in fact, our love for Lt. Columbo affirms this. Because on the show ... they don't get away with it.

Most of us do not begrudge people their money. In fact, in the good news/bad news department, we aspire to it.

But we don't want them to receive special treatment *because* of it. And yes, we've been known to give them that special treatment ourselves … and yes, we want that money, along with a special life, too … if we ever get that cash.

But the show is there — the lieutenant is there — to remind us it's wrong.

We don't care if they own a BMW. But. If they push it off a cliff, with their spouse (already dead) behind the wheel, and pretend it was a kidnapping gone awry, and try to weasel their way out of it, and lie like a bad toupee — we want the bastards nailed.

*

I now have the entire collection, all 35 years, nearly 70 episodes in all, and I've seen each of them at least twice, most of them more than that, and a few favorites nearing 10 times apiece.

For this book, I watched every episode in Season One again, and then again. I must confess — it is after all an essay about the truth and its tendency to will out — that this got harder, as I went. Because in watching closely to write the best guide I could, I had to look at the shows — writing, acting, and even Mr. Falk — differently. Among other differences, I looked more closely. And at a few points I grew weary; there was discomfort and dreariness.

But the tighter angles and heavier analysis also showed me why we watch.

Why we watch at all, and why we keep watching — and why it matters — even if we can't *say* why, and don't need to know to like it more and more each time. The qualities that draw us in, and keep us there, are the ones that bloom, that burrow deep, without our even noticing.

*

It's because it's true.

The *Columbo* we love — and the Columbo we love to watch annoy hell out of the murderers, until some of them beg to be caught and taken away just so the questions will stop — all of it stems from the deep truths of stories — and about human nature itself.

There's the restoration of order of course, order of many kinds, and there's the reminder to the rich that the rule of the universe is you get what you need not what you think you deserve and that even money and power and your supposedly foolproof plan cannot protect you, if you kill.

There is how Lt. Columbo solves the crime, which we the eyewitnesses have seen: namely by gamely paying attention and asking questions. Those are deep practices not unrelated to love.

There is also his essential kindness: how even when he's tracking the killer — even we know he knows and that realization is slowly dawning on the murderer, too … he's unfailingly … nice.

He is nearly unfailingly good.

Lt. Columbo is — to use words said to be more in demand today than 40 years ago, but that are actually ever-welcome — genuine, authentic, and real. He actually *is* intrigued (to take an actual example, from Episode 1:2) about what to do when decorative soap sticks together after it's used.

When he notices stuff it's not that he's being annoying, or that he's weird. These are quirks, odd, whatchamacallit … idiosyncrasies … even to us … but that's because we're not that consistently questioning, caring, and kind.

I think he truly is intrigued, curious — even at times in *wonder* — about such things.

When in every episode, every … single … one … he notices at least a half-dozen details, niggling crummy little curiosities, it's because he really wants to know. Of course — at times he's showing the murderer the game is not only afoot, but that it's almost up.

But he also knows *life isn't like that*, or shouldn't be, and what we just saw just doesn't fit … and why not?

He knows it should be otherwise, and if it's not, something's wrong and needs to be righted.

And of course it's because the account of life the murderer gives — from who they blame for all their ills, to what they say, to how they leave the crime scene, to how they behave afterward, and the explanations they give for all of this — is utterly false.

*

The reason it works is because it's true and real and deep. And this is possible because the writers knew — know — Lt. Columbo, and everything about him.

The facts aren't as important as the truth. There are inconsistencies over the series in the show's telling of the man: whether he can cook, let's say, whether he drinks, and even about his beloved missus. But the truth, as ever, lives on well past the facts.

And so does *Columbo*.

The writers know everything about Lt. Columbo ... Peter Falk knew ... and now, at any time, we can too.

*

Peter Falk died June 23, 2011. The obituaries began June 24, 2011 — my fifth wedding anniversary.

Still married and still watching, I also confess to liking 1970s episodes the most: the ones I saw as a kid, the ones with all the kitsch. I may simply be too close to episodes from the 1980s and 1990s: too close to the parachute pants and mullets, too close to the techno-music. Maybe an overacting killer embarrasses me when it's from the years I came of age. The 1970s just seem more like fun.

And *Columbo* is a joy to watch, no matter what the year.

And that's why we do.

Gee, That's Funny …

The wicked women of Columbo

In "Ransom for a Dead Man" (1:2), murderer Leslie Williams takes Lt. Columbo up in a plane. The policeman is not fond of heights, to say the least. At one point she asks,

"Are you afraid of flying?"

"Well, it's not one my favorite pastimes," he says.

"It's a great release for me, lieutenant," she says. "Being up here, all alone, totally free."

Erica Jong's *Fear of Flying* would not be published until 1973; this episode aired in 1971. But if we don't have here "art imitating art," we might have two examples of art imitating life.

For in conventional terms, these were reflections of American life as women asserted their own bad selves, entered the workforce, and began to do many things previously reserved for men — including kill people.

In two of Season One's nine episodes, women kill. In two others, they are key to a male criminal's plan — and in one of those, she is also key to Columbo's then trapping the male murderer.

In yet another there are two strong female characters, one particularly so. In a sixth, the witness is a woman, weak, but starting to emerge as an independent voice. While in a seventh the victim is a woman (so you could argue she winds up dead for being assertive) but her attacker is shown in the end as the weaker of the two

Not to mention a sonofabitch, found out and caught by that weakness: his hubris and his rage.

So in only two of nine episodes ["Murder by the Book" (1:3) and "Short Fuse" (1:8)] are the female characters especially irrelevant — mere foils for the men on stage.

I don't suggest the show was created and written to accomplish all the above, and aggressively attack opposing positions. But seven of nine episodes include plot components doing just that.

Women in the first season of *Columbo* are strong, willful, and resilient, even the murderesses, even when they're caught. To be sure, some of it now appears heavy-handed — future seasons get even campy in spots — and there is some speechifying. But at the time, it was big.

Women are wealthy and powerful, attorneys and executives, and they hardly need a man at all, unless it's to shoot him in his home. They don't want to be married, married at all, or marriage.

We see women being catty, as well as cooperating with each other to trap the male killer (1:1); they fight, with others and each other (1:2), and even the latter tells us both female characters want something and will battle for it; they stick to their guns, no pun intended (1:5); they seize corporate power (1:7).

They also use and enjoy their sexuality. Without any effort I can think of elements of this in five of the nine episodes — especially but not limited to interacting with the lieutenant. In some, the power definitely derives from their uniqueness as women.

We shouldn't make overly much of this. The story, as I said a moment ago, is king — even when it's queen. But there is something going on here, already in this first season. In the infancy of the new show, the makers and presenters show exponential expansion in a particular view of woman. It's amazing to watch.

The Episodes

Note

The first *Columbo* is "Prescription: Murder" —
generally considered a separate movie, and
listed by the Internet Movie Database as one.
Then "Ransom for a Dead Man" is the pilot
and "Murder by the Book" comes in at Episode
1 (1:1).

This is two off my numbering. That's part of
why I've followed the Season One DVD
collection, which simply includes all of the
episodes, in order, starting with "Prescription:
Murder."

Keying to the DVDs also gets us more
involved in actually watching the shows, not
just talking about them — at least until DVDs
don't exist anymore.

Plus, the DVDs are eventually the only way to
make sense of things. As *Columbo* grew more
popular, it morphed from its original series
into an occasional TV movie, and they made
fewer each year. The last "season" (#13 on
DVD) actually spans eight years (1995-2003)
and for only 5 episodes.

Prescription: Murder

Episode 1:1

The Players

Killer: Gene Barry

Victim: Nina Foch

Director: Richard Irving

Writers: Richard Levinson, William Link

Columbo comes on stage 32 minutes in, 1/3 of into a 99 minutes run time, and presaging his 'late' arrival always: murders in *Columbo* are 15 to 25 minutes old by the time he shows. And since episodes go to 75 minutes after the first two (the original series had a 90-minute time slot) that's one-fifth to one-third of the way done before he's introduced. Must have been incredible with the original play doing that.

Gene Barry's secretary is Virginia Gregg, whose voice is the mother in "Psycho." William Windom, who plays Barry's attorney friend, and pressures Columbo to lay off the investigation, was a veteran character actor in Hollywood for more than 55 years — in fact he'll re-appear in 1:8 "Short Fuse" — and died only recently, in 2012. Gene Barry and Nina Foch lived at least into their 80s: Foch died in 2008; Barry in 2009. Peter Falk died in 2011.

The Show

Gene Barry played dapper lawmen in "Bat Masterson" and "Burke's Law" — and plays a dapper villain named Ray Flemming who kills his wealthy wife. Barry reps the suave wing of the 1960s, while a sharp Dave Grusin soundtrack trips about among psychedelic inkblots over the opening credits. This is an episode *of* the 1960s — character in 1960, play in 1964, TV episode in 1968 — and we feel it. One of the opening credit inkblots is the first card in the official Rorschach test, a dominant diagnostic of that decade.

Flemming is a sociopath, committing adultery on his 10th wedding anniversary (and many times before) while declining to answer his mistress when she asks if he loves her. He's purely material — equating courage with "a strong central nervous system." And when our man calls it murder, Flemming is genuinely shocked to see Columbo be so judgmental. He says it's not insanity but pragmatism, and even when Columbo catches him, the bastard remains resolute. He should die.

Some Quirks include a marginally employed actress who at some point went to see a highly-powered psychiatrist, though we can be pretty sure he's no longer charging her for services; a socialite wife in preparation for a trip who does not go to the hairdresser or shop for a new outfit; the suggestion of an amorous (for her) encounter on a bed far too small for it; light strangulation alone as murder method (unreliable to say the least); and some fast-and-loose ersatz medical theories: "We're hoping she wakes up long enough to tell us something" — i.e., just before she dies.

The *Recurring Elements* are technically none; it's the first episode. But we'll see psychiatrists and mind-experts as killers again, for sure.

Loveable Columbo items include how he forgets things, multiple comments on his environment (couch, lighter, the lighter's flame). Elements that do *not* become emblematic include Columbo being nearly dapper — white shirt pressed, tie knotted, suit neat, combed short hair ... so young! Later he even wears a buff blue shirt! He also shouts at the mistress, growing increasingly angry with her: a most un-Columbo-like behavior.

Best Scene

Cat and mouse in Flemming's office, discussing a "hypothetical" killer Columbo is chasing. Also good: the pool scene and not just for the polka dot bikinis in abundance. The scene in each show where Lt. Columbo and the killer sit and joust with purpose is always good and sometimes best.

Worst Scene

When the doctor gives the news, *we* all know whodunit; now we wonder why *they* all don't know too. Second worst is "angry elf" acting: the stock "troubled youth" character: clunky.

Quotes

"What about that man — that Columbo?"

"People don't always do the rational thing."

"He'd look for flaws in the Old Testament."

"We're in love. We want a future together. That's all the justification we need."

"Listen I'm sorry about all this, doctor — I seem to be making a pest of myself."

"Maybe I hired someone to kill her. That boy who confessed — maybe I paid him to do it."
"No doc, you didn't do that."
"How do you know?"
"I already asked him."

"The astonishing thing is you're likable. Has anyone ever told you you're droll?"

"I haven't given you a Rorschach test yet, but I've got a hunch you're a bourbon man."

"[The murderer] he's got just one time to learn — just one. With us [cops] it's a business: we do this a hundred times a year. I'll tell ya doc: that's a lot of practice."

Ransom for a Dead Man

Episode 1:2

The Players

Killer: Lee Grant

Victim: Harlan Warde

Director: Richard Irving

Writer: Dean Hargrove

Columbo appears 15 minutes into the 95-minute episode, or about one-sixth in. The official "pilot" of the series, made three years after "Prescription: Murder" and airing in 1971, it's the second episode on DVD.

At this writing, Lee Grant is still alive, aged 85. She's the mother of Dinah Manoff, who's best known for TV shows "Soap" and "Empty Nest," co-starring with Richard Mulligan in both cases. Grant had already won an Academy Award by the time she guest starred on *Columbo*: quite a coup to have her be the first official killer. She would later be nominated three more times for Academy Awards, winning twice.

Timothy Carey appears as Bert who runs Barney's Beanery. Carey did two others: once more as Bert, this season in "Dead Weight" (1:5), then as a witness, Tony, in "Fade in to

Murder" (6:1). In 1976 he acted in "The Killing of a Chinese Bookie," directed by Peter Falk's pal John Cassavetes and starring Ben Gazzara.

Falk, Cassavetes, and Gazzara were good friends. Cassavetes would kill in "Étude in Black" (2:1) and Ben Gazzara directed two episodes, "A Friend in Deed" (3:8) and "Troubled Waters" (4:4).

Harold Gould plays a supporting role as an FBI agent. Gould was a college professor with a Ph.D. before he began acting in his 40s. Like many *Columbo* actors, he lived well into his 80s, dying in 2010.

The Show

They still haven't settled on a font for the credits, but from the minute we see a woman's hands pasting together the ransom note, we know we're in for something different. Lee Grant plays Leslie Williams, a high-powered attorney who kills her husband. Ach! Those scissors, snipping the reel-to-reel tape! Love that the daughter watches the movie "Double Indemnity." Never saw Barbara Stanwyck on *Columbo* ...

Some Quirks include the killer badly feigning ignorance of the use of the phone technology she has used to concoct her alibi — and which she'd previously shown to the lieutenant. By then her saying "Want to explain to me how you did it?" is hard to accept. Sending a homicide lieutenant as the local police liaison seems off, too.

I want to complain about the very 1970s décor — bright, gaudy, whites, silvers, gold — and the slew of freaky-deaky TV practices of the time (jarring noises, camera shots, one part of a scene (her eyes) disappearing into another (car headlights), repeated during the phony ransom drop, too. But whatya gonna do?

Recurring Elements here are breaking a trust to get money, as in "The Greenhouse Jungle" (2:2), shooting the victim in his living room: cf. "Suitable for Framing" (1:6), though of course there are only so many places to kill someone; a briefcase left briefly on a couch, as Flemming's grey glove on the bar (1:1). Look also for Columbo getting the inadvertent final clue tying it all together. It happens w/Bert.

In the *Loveable Columbo* behavior this time, he's more rumpled, as we will come to expect. Not totally, but the tie is a bit more flyaway and the trench coat wrinkled, and the transformation will be complete in 1:3. He tells about a family member "I have this cousin Ralph" and we can see this is going to be part of the show.

And there he is, asking third parties — boyfriends, servants, and other cops — why a killer is doing this or that, contrary to what most people would do. The lieutenant is usually (but not always) right about this.

He also uses a lighter on the desk (cf. 1:1), loses his pen, is barely and dismissively acknowledged by "the authorities," and is utterly clueless (initially) about technology.

Best Scene

It's fun to watch him afraid of heights and I always enjoy the "idiosyncrasy" dialogue, where the two actors seem to be ad-libbing, it's done so well. But the enduring scenes are where Columbo shows genuine concern for Mrs. Williams, even as he becomes sure of her guilt. She does not deserve his kindness, but she still needs it. Also check Gould's FBI agent threatening to "take it upstairs" — and Columbo putting him in his place, calmly.

Worst Scene

The mother-daughter catfights are shrill and sharp and too melodramatic.

Quotes

"You fly a plane?"
"Yes."
"By yourself?"
"Yes."

"No kidding?"
"No kidding."

"You know the soap you have in the bathroom, the ones shaped like little lemons? Well I was almost afraid to use 'em."
"But that's what they're there for, lieutenant — to be used."
"Well if you don't mind my asking: when you use one, and you put it back in the plate, how do you keep it from sticking to the others?"
"It's a problem."
"That's what I figured."

"You know, today they could do everything electronically, if they wanted to. I'd bet on that."

"They got a new thing today. If I wanna take my wife to the ballgame, I just dial this service. For the tickets. It's all done by the computer. It's unbelievable."

"With me, I'm a strange guy."
"Really?"
"Yeah, little things bother me. I'm a worrier. … my wife, she says to me, you can really be a pain. You know what I mean."
"Yeah, I get the general picture."

"See, I'm trying to show you a whatchamacallit of mine … "
"An idiosyncrasy."
"Right. Idiosyncrasy. Gee that's a good word."
"Oh, one of the best."

"Ah, Mrs. Williams — would you not do that."
"You're nervous."
"No offense, but it's like being in the car. I'm always nervous when I'm not driving."

"I could teach you how to handle the plane, in an hour."
"Well, really, that would be wasted on me. I don't intend to fly again."

"Do you like it?"
"I'd appreciate if we didn't talk for awhile."

"I'm sorry I can't be more help."
"No it's alright. You've helped."

"You know what you're trouble is, you don't have much imagination. You always order the chili."

Murder by the Book

Episode 1:3

The Players

Killer: Jack Cassidy

Victims: Martin Milner, Barbara Colby

Director: Steven Spielberg

Writer: Steven Bochco

Columbo enters 18 minutes in; the episode is 76 minutes long. For the first, two, the show ran two hours: a stand-alone movie and a pilot. Now the show is in its 90-minute slot, with about 15 minutes committed for commercials. This episode first aired six months after (1:2).

The show marks the first appearance of Jack Cassidy, father of Sean and David Cassidy, and ex-husband of Shirley Jones. He would go on to play two other killers in *Columbo*: see "Publish or Perish" (3:5) and "Now You See Him" (5:5). He died before age 50, in an accidental fire.

Spielberg said this work got him "Duel" — his first major movie — starring Dennis Weaver, who played *McCloud*, a second of the shows in the original version of NBC's Mystery Movie rotation, with *Columbo* and *McMillan and Wife*.

Steven Bochco became story editor for *Columbo*, and went on to create many TV shows, including *Hill Street Blues*, *L.A. Law*, and *NYPD Blue*.

Barbara Colby was later the victim of a real-life murder.

The Show

Mystery novel writing partners Jim Ferris (Milner) and Ken Franklin (Cassidy) are breaking up. So the latter ices the former, which won't bring the lucrative writing team back together but will satisfy other, deeper tendencies than mere writing. There is humor in this set-up, in that Richard Levinson and William Link are writing partners who make mysteries.

Interesting point in the opening scene, where Ferris is typing and he misspells "J'Acuse" … can't decide if that's purposeful (authors aren't always good spelers) or not. Juxtapose it with Franklin, driving up in his Bentley (or Rolls?). The one is working; the other is playing.

The episode is also notable for some practices you don't see often today, such as people stating addresses and/or phone numbers. They aren't real of course (least I don't think so), but they do sound more real than today, when it's all "555-1234" and there's no imagination at all.

You'd think they'd come up with a standard fake phone number or address — one that might actually *do something* even. A web URL in an early episode of "Breaking Bad" led to a cancer-fighting donation page.

In any event, Franklin lives at "937 Skyview Drive" he says. It's only filmed at night in this one, and I'm told the same set is used in "The Most Crucial Game" (2:3) as the victim's house.

Some Quirks begin when Franklin reaches into his glove compartment for his gun — where we all keep them, especially here in California. I wish I could say the interviewer's terrible softball questions were fake; I am afraid they're very much true-to-life.

Quirky but not necessarily false is arrogant Cassidy mentioning a "bill of indictment" (to let us know he knows) and suing for "false arrest and defamation of character." Can you even do that? Ah the threats of Ken Franklin, a fundamentally weak man.

That the two partners "met in a typewriter shop" — well, it's just awesome. And weird, now.

Franklin's closing line "You want to know the irony of all this? That is my idea. The only really good one I ever had. I must have told it to Jim five years ago. Whoever thought that idiot would write it down?" is a classic in not knowing what to say to wrap it all up. Because really, whoever thought a writer — who was said to scribble every little idea on scraps of paper and random napkins — would write something down?

More curiosities include a horsey-looking second victim with great legs. Also look for the Mrs. Melville book, *Perfect Alibi*, which I'd make even money came from the L&L idea factory. And who knew "dossiers" were a big deal in 1971? Franklin says Ferris was "compiling dossiers" and in a second episode this season — "Short Fuse" (1:8) I think — another character asks about them.

Shh!!!

Recurring Elements are the messy second murder — though interestingly enough Columbo is wrong when he says the first murder was Ferris's idea (for a Mrs. Melville book) and the second was Franklin being sloppy. A foreshadowing clue, however, involves the victim's wife telling of ideas written on scraps of paper — which the lieutenant eventually finds. Though there are no psychiatrists in this one, a character does refer to "analysis without the couch."

Lovable Columbo behaviors has our man getting a receipt for two hot dogs, loosening his tie even more all the way through, and being very kind, this time to the wife of the victim. There's some confusion for the makers, at this point, perhaps, when Lt. Columbo drinks with Franklin in his home, when the body's "discovered." In (1:7) Columbo will say off-handedly at one point that he doesn't drink. But overall, he does. Ray Flemming (1:1) says he's a bourbon man —something of a cut, I think. Columbo also claims he's the worst cook in the world, which in later shows will never be heard again: he's Italian, and an excellent cook.

Best Scene

Coolest bits for me were the scenes with no dialogue, and very little sound: the opening credits, over which a typewriter and music plays; or when Franklin rows to the middle of the lake; or in closing credits. Spielberg is clearly in charge here, applying his cinematic sense to television.

Worst Scene

Sometimes I find supercilious, arrogant prick Cassidy always plays in *Columbo* to be a pain; sometimes it's fun and campy. You should know it might feel the former. All the killers the lieutenant faces are arrogant.

Cassidy overplays it, for several scenes, and he's a lousy killer (the champagne cork, for instance) so it's not even justified. Maybe Mr. Franklin should have helped his partner more on the books.

Quotes

"What I like about these new machines is you don't have to push a button. They go off by the heat of your hands."

"Believe me, I'm very grateful for all the help you've given me."

"Is there any chance of our having a drink together?"
"I'd love to really, but you see the young lady and I are going to have a late supper."
"I think you might want to cancel it."

"Perhaps under better circumstances — less-harassed circumstances — I could give you a more detailed interview ... even in more depth."
"Oh that'd be nice. Shall I call you?"

"The lady detective! What a character — what a brain! And what logic, the way she figures it out!"

"I'm sorry — I'm making a pest of myself."
"Naww — "
"Yes, yes, I am. It's because I keep asking these questions, but I tell ya, I can't help myself. It's a habit."

"Unless you just want to take a second, to know how we're progressing on your partner's list."

"Oh? Anything concrete?"
"No. Not a thing."

"By itself it doesn't prove anything."

"Mrs. Ferris, it wouldn't matter if you knew him for a hundred years. That wouldn't change anything. This man Franklin took your husband's life."

"Last night I called to tell you I was coming. But there was no one at home."

Death Lends a Hand

Episode 1:4

The Players

Killer: Robert Culp

Victim: Patricia Crowley

Director: Bernard L. Kowalski

Writers: Levinson & Link

At 17 minutes in, Columbo appears: he's being pulled over for a ticket. Inlcude this episode, Falk dueled Culp four times in *Columbo*. Culp played the murderer in two others ["The Most Crucial Game (2:3) and "Double Exposure" (3:4)] and the father of a killer in a 1990 entry "Columbo Goes to College" (10:1). Culp killers were sharp tongued and natty, with penchants for double-breasted suits. He died in 2010, at age 79, after falling outside his home.

Ray Milland is Arthur Kennicut, the victim's husband, who would play a murderer the following season in "The Greenhouse Jungle" (2:2).

The Show

After Culp's character, a private detective named Brimmer, inadvertently kills

Kennicut's wife, the lieutenant must show how, and even why.

This when people still wore vests with their suits, and drove immense cars. But it seems unlikely that a security expert would leave his terrace door unlooked. Especially since at least some of the liaisons may have happened nearby, which Brimmer surely knew. Also, he threatens to go return to Kennicut and say, *I lied to you so I could blackmail your wife*, which I rather doubt.

Meanwhile, Mrs. Kennicut makes *the* classic TV mistake of telling a bad guy everything you're going to. Of course, she didn't know he was going to crush her skull. After he does, he takes her ring to make it look like a robbery, and isn't wearing gloves. But the overall scene is very cool, with Brimmer looking into the camera, and viewers watching his actions in the lenses of his glasses.

Some Quirks include Columbo pushing the kid on the swing; not incorrect but it jars us today, doesn't it? Today it'd be creepy and the mother would call the cops. At another point, Brimmer notes Columbo's "convoluted mind" … then compliments his thinking and offers to hire him. Neither statement is honest, but together they don't even make sense.

Culp's Brimmer merits special mention: he's excellent. The terseness speaking, in actions — he is precise, cutting, and careful, and not careful enough. He draws out elements of the character slowly, though not always (see "Worst Scene"). You'll like watching him not bust out laughing when Falk is into his patter. Brimmer's mobile number is 476-7301, most likely in the (213) area code.

Recurring Elements here include Columbo using a lighter in someone's office (he does that *all* the time), asking an expert (a golf pro here) for "help" so he can ask more questions, the massive cars, and lush homes: Kennicut's backyard looks suspiciously like the old Getty Center. Then again, a lot of California does.

The *Loveable Columbo* starts asking questions fast, when first with Brimmer and Kennicut. The questions show Brimmer that Columbo already knows things (e.g., golf clubs in the closet; I think the lieutenant opened it "wrong" on purpose, to see inside).

Columbo is always noticing, always asking questions — and he's audacious about it, as when he looks in the golf pro's appointment book. This time he's at the DMV when he gets that *one clue* that ties it all together.

At the end he tells of "the old neighborhood" ... as the music begins ... and the credits roll.

Best Scene

Columbo pretends to read palms. He looks at Kennicut's and Brimmer's hands. As with many of his tics and behaviors, this is a 'tell' that's partly offered to 'show' others the lieutenant's a doofus. In this case it also gives him important evidence of Brimmer's guilt. 'Nother good'un is Columbo interviewing the golf pro, and letting him know that he knows his secret by asking about people who might have been on the make with the victim.

Worst Scene

The several minutes where the young associate in Brimmer's firm shows Columbo around. The boss goes *way* overboard berating him — rivaling Jack Cassidy's cheez and showing he has that nasty temper ... which Columbo has just said is an aspect of the killer's personality. Then, after the dressing down, the kid gives away even more secrets, which he definitely would *not* do.

Quotes

"This one's as crooked as a dog's hind leg."

"Mr. Kennicut isn't here yet."
"Well he's not due for another 30 seconds."

"Say, are you a cop?"

"I hope the association will be beneficial to you."
"Oh, I'm sure it will."

"You know, I suddenly feel very much more optimistic about this whole thing."

"This is your appointment book isn't it?"
"You should know — you've been looking at it."

"From what I see, you gave her a lot of lessons."
"She liked the game."

"Hey, listen: can I help you out? Don't say anything else. You don't have an attorney. Wait until you get an attorney. This way, you can hurt your case. Believe me. I know something about my business."

"Did you find anything?"
"No, not really. Well ... "

"I don't think a man kills with his hands unless he's angry."

"Turning on the ladies is about the only thing I do well. I'm not a very good golfer."

"You didn't kill her."
"I know that, but — "

"Well, Arthur, I don't like to be critical. But ... "

"Oh certainly. You'll be the first to know."

"We're lucky Lenore lost this."
"Um, she didn't lose it."

"I got a feeling the reason I became a cop was to make up for all those jokes I played when I was a kid."

Dead Weight

Episode 1:5

The Players

Killer: Eddie Albert

Victim: John Kerr

Director: Jack Smight

Writer: John T. Dugan

Lt. Columbo appears 11 minutes in, which is quick for him. Perhaps they needed more time to complete the arc of the witness recanting, then coming back to reality, but more story development in the beginning wd have been welcome, instead of verbally explaining the general's problem so much. It's the first episode of *Columbo* scoring below 7 on IMDB.

Timothy Carey returns as Burt, and his WWII memorabilia give Lt. Columbo the final clue. Val Avery, who became a regular horse in the stable of actors for the show, is here for the first time, as the guy renting the boats. Avery was Armenian, acted for decades, and died in 2009 at age 85.

The story about someone stealing a general's pistol while he was recuperating in hospital, was played out in an episode of "M*A*S*H" as well; that show launched a year after this one.

Real-life newsman Clete Roberts plays a news broadcaster on the television Columbo and Bert watch. He later played a news journalist in "M*A*S*H" as well.

Suzanne Pleshette, the witness, began her role in "The Bob Newhart Show" in 1972.

The Show

Helen Stewart (Pleshette) witnesses Major General Martin J. Hollister (Albert) kill a colonel with whom he has been bilking the government. Military cost over-runs did not originate in the 1980s. Commensurate with the age, the army gets dinged often during *Columbo*. But the lieutenant is generally supportive — until the murder intrudes.

Some Quirks include a very cowardly cop; this is also a *Recurring Element* because policemen in the series are always deferring to the criminal and his or her demands. It's so common that it has got to be a feature, not a bug; my guess is it helps establish the killer's position and arrogance.

[Kinda puts in perspective later cop shows where they interrogate people who never ever ask for an attorney. Revenge is sweet.]

Other *Quirks* include the "Marine Military Institute" (not a bad fake name) and Gen. Hollister in a Victor Kiam impression with the electric razor. Helen Stewart's home phone number is 985-4321 — more than likely in the (714) area code (at that time), since they're boating on Balboa Bay. She lives with Mother at 8090 Vail. All of this would be near enough to the Newport geographically — and a million miles away, based on money.

[But it's not supposed to *be* OC, of course, since an L.A. police lieutenant investigates.]

More problematic is why a smart guy like the general wouldn't just take off for a couple days, sail hundreds of miles out to sea, and dump the body where it never would wash ashore. [And that colonel should have called the general instead … like he wanted to. ☺]

Eddie Albert plays Hollister's annoyance well: he's a general and used to getting his way. But it seems off he would then also be ripping off the military, which he's fond of? Did he feel forced out? More backstory please! He also is well versed in sailing and military terminology, and one dapper dude — vanity, vanity.

Recurring Elements include Columbo talking apparently idly, but actually to show the criminal he's more than a little onto him. The general shows an array of guns, for instance, but Columbo asks after a pistol, and gets the general to lie about his favored gun — which becomes vital. He later brings up how trouble "back at the department" forces him to continue working the case.

The cop who won't question the general is the means for the lieutenant to come on the scene. It also creates the scene where they mistake Columbo for a guy who shouldn't be there at all.

Loveable Columbo is complimenting Helen Stewart who, to say the least, doesn't think highly of herself. He also tells of brother-in-law George, who advised him to go fishing ... then he asks about the gun. In this one we learn Columbo doesn't like boats either.

He gave the general a chance to actually confess, right at the end, but the general doesn't take it. And because Columbo wants Helen to understand the man — he builds the case against him.

If you know Poe's "The Purloined Letter" you enjoy the solution that much more.

Best Scene

When Columbo and Hollister are bantering about fishing, a metaphor for pursuing a murderer. There's also a good gradual development of the witness' change from "I saw it" to "I didn't see it" because of the general's attentions. But I wouldn't want to be her therapist after this.

The gulls screeching instead of the gunshot is nice.

Worst Scene

Any scene with the mother; no single one is horrible, but taken together, she's vile. Denigrating her daughter, taking her philandering ex-son-in-law's side, etc. What if someone were actually *like* that in real life … it'd be hard to like the show, because they're using this thing you desperately hope is a caricature, to further a plot. The ramifications stagger.

Hollister's denials and denunciations are a also little weak when they're on the boat — though he is very much in control, and more so by the time they return to the dock.

Quotes

"I'm down at the boat place."

"Do you know who lives in that house?"
"No. Does it matter?"

"Oh yes — I remember now."

"Who reported this uh, this murder."
"Now, I never said it was murder."
"Well, this alleged shooting. Who turned in the report?"
"I'm afraid I can't tell you that, General. Against regulations."
"Well … whoever it was, it had to be some guy on a boat in the marina."

"General, I'd like to keep the record straight on that. I never said that it was a man."
"Well then it was a woman."
"Well now, I never said that either."
"OK, it doesn't make any difference."

"Mother is the eternal optimist. She's always hoping for the worst."

"Does it sound like a reasonable explanation?"
"Oh, very reasonable. But it's not what I saw."

"Mrs. Stewart, a murder charge is about as serious as you can get."
"I didn't ask you if it was a serious charge. I asked you if you believe me."

"Just a piece of advice. Find a different spot. Or use different bait. Otherwise, you're not going to catch anything, lieutenant."

"It strikes me that *you're* the one who downgrades yourself. One dinner with General Hollister, and you begin to doubt your senses."

"Those were my plumper days. My mother said I looked like a radish."

"Any idea what happened?"
"Yessir. Somebody shot him."

"I don't see how a man with the name Columbo — shouldn't he be more at home on a boat?"
"Musta been another branch of the family, sir. How soon before we land?"

"He thinks I shot him."
"What I think is unimportant. What's
important is what you saw."
"I didn't see anything."

"Some men, lieutenant, do not want to look
like an unmade bed."

"If it was me, if it was my gun, I would take
very good care of that gun. I'd have it in my
apartment, where people could see it. And I
would keep it polished. And I would keep it
oiled. And I would keep it loaded. ... And
that's the gun that I would use."

"Where is the gun?"

"Do you really have a niece?"
"What kind of a question is that?"
"Well do you?"
"Of course I've got a niece: my wife's sister's
girl, Cynthia."

Suitable for Framing

Episode 1:6

The Players

Killer: Ross Martin

Victims: Robert Shayne, Rosanna Huffman

Director: Hy Averback

Writer: Jackson Gillis

Columbo enters 14 minutes in, directly on to the investigation of the murder. It's not the first episode with two murders [that was "Murder by the Book" (1:3)] and it won't be the last. As for this practice, it usually involves a very sloppy second killing, as it does here.

This one brims with TV and movie staples and stalwarts: Martin played Robert Conrad's sidekick Artemus Gordon in "The Wild, Wild West;" Conrad is the killer in "An Exercise in Fatality" (4:1).

Robert Shayne, briefly here, was a longtime B-movie actor. Kim Hunter as Aunt Edna is known for "Planet of the Apes" [Her costar in that, Roddy McDowall, will kill soon in (1:8)]. The lawyer Don Ameche was a 1930s & 1940s leading man, and ½ of "The Bickersons".

In lesser roles, Barney Phillips is a police captain; he's the second alien in that classic "Twilight Zone" set in a diner, where two invasions of earth are pending. Vic Tayback, the painter, is Mel, in "Alice."

This is the first of 11 *Columbo* episodes Jackson Gillis wrote. He died at age 93, in 2010.

Several of the paintings in the first scene show up in other episodes of the series.

The Show

Dale Kingston murders his uncle Rudy, because he's learned he won't inherit the art collection. He tries to pin the murder on Aunt Edna, divorced many years earlier from Rudy. He also kills Tracy O'Connor, who helped with the first murder. This one can't be pinned on Edna — mainly because it sucks.

Many episodes start with a huge house, a shot of the exterior, a wealthy someone in the way, and the murder. Again I like (this may even qualify as a *Recurring Element*) how Kingston plants all the evidence and arranges the crime scene without speaking — barely any sound at all. The only actual non-soundtrack noise is the piano and the gunshot ... and then the doorbell.

He looks at his watch multiple times. This can be seen as "over-the-top" behavior (we viewers are to see him and know he's arranging his alibi) but it's also good evidence of his nature: he thinks his plan is awesome, and going like clockwork; moreover he thinks others should hop to, when he wants them to. He looks at his watch at the scene, in his car, during his terrible jokes ... he is a guy who would be obsessively checking Facebook.

Some Quirks ... where does the blood go when you shoot someone? We almost never see it. And while it must be fun to wreck a room, the supposed thief is supposed to be after the art, so why'd he trash the place at all? In this case, the murderer doesn't think to wonder whether the cops will wonder why that alarm didn't go off ... even though they always ask about it.

At least he dresses for dinner and murder: a velvet jacket — though I can't see why the girl had to wear boots to run down stone steps.

If you're wondering whether police lieutenants directly investigate crimes, you can also wonder about this one, in which a captain personally attends at several points.

Kingston calls the missing Degas ballet dancers "paintings" and his accomplice says, "I want to paint like that." Do we call pastels "paintings?" In the art category generally, I love that during the gallery show the price of a painting goes from $1,000 to $800 when the buyer balks ... then back to $1,200 when the famous critic shows. The show nails the falsity of this behavior. See also "Quotes."

In the last scene, an apple falls on the floor when they clear the table. Nobody picks it up. And the address of the house is 417 Pine View, in Bel Air.

Recurring Elements include Columbo forgetting something (the paintings) and nearly leaving with the lawyer's lighter. Like the mistress in (1:1) a woman asks Kingston to reassure her of his love. Like Flemming in (1:1), he's less than emphatic. Columbo almost lights a stogie in Wealthy Art Patron's house, earning a scolding from the domestic staff. This will happen again.

The solution is similar to "A Friend In Deed" (3:8), and Columbo meeting Kingston at the studio is a Universal "set as a set." They discuss meeting later at the house, similar to (1:1) when he and Flemming agree to meet up, and both end up there, but not as planned. And are those the *very* same grey gloves Flemming used to kill his wife?

Instead of using a lighter on a desk, Columbo asks about the coffee machine in the TV studio. Signature verification by "the boys at the lab" is a huge deal in police procedurals of the time.

We *Love Columbo* when he asks about the grapes, "are they real?" He SHOUTS!!! at the crime scene, with a total lack of decorum; he just wants to solve the crime. He's nervous around nudity, and apologetic for pestering

Kingston — who is then apoplectic when the lieutenant accepts his offer of a house key.

He's kind again, this time to Aunt Edna who is sweet and addled and chirpy: a female Columbo.

Best Scene

Lt. Columbo looking at the photo album with the landlady, played by Mary Wickes: a hilarious scene. The facial tics, the nodding, the pauses and interplay are so good.

Worst Scene

Ross Martin kissing the girl, and the second murder. Both are gruesome. It gets worse when he starts some really unskilled reverse psychologizing —with only 15 minutes left as a free man.

Quotes

"It's just my uncle. I assure you he's far more amiable now than he ever was when he was alive."

"The only thing I really need is something pink for the guest bathroom."

"What's the matter? Haven't you seen people without faces before?"

"Pastels? You mean like the kids use in school?"
"Nobody used pastels like Degas, lieutenant!"

"I don't think I understand."
"You know what, that's the trouble: I don't think I do either."

"Can you imagine he thinks the artist should decide what goes in the painting!?"

"When you take the 'w' off of 'wart' you're still left with art."

"So this is a television studio, huh? Quite a place."

"Things aren't really what they seem, are they?"

"I'm gonna tell you something. Do you know that there is a reasonable explanation for everything, if you just put your mind to it."

"Why can't I paint like that?"

"I told you that you had talent when you first came to see me."
"Sometimes I think my talent is what you like best about me."
"Well it's a combination of things, really."

"What are you doing here at this hour of the night?"
"Is it night?"

"This girl Tracy O'Connor, who'd she go out with? C'mon tell me. She dated, didn't she?"

"Oh she was talented."
"She's a very gifted girl."
"Darn right."

"That's awful cute — I made her that dress ...
doesn't that look nice? See that's smocking."

"Oh look at that one too, isn't that a good one?
That was taken at the zoo. That's a good one of
the lion."

"I'm still convinced Aunt Edna had nothing to
do with this."
"You know, I think I agree with you."

"I don't want to go around pointing my finger
at anyone, until I have an airtight case."

"Sorry, you can't go in there."

"Gee they're something aren't they? Pastels,
you know."

"Suppose you ... "

Lady in Waiting

Episode 1:7

The Players

Killer: Susan Clark

Victim: Richard Anderson

Director: Norman Lloyd

Writers: Steven Bochco, Barney Slater, Ted Leighton

Columbo comes in 21 minutes into the episode and finds the newspaper right away, finding also no good answer for why it's there. First appearance of Fred Draper: he's the cab driver here, and will play in five other episodes, including one as the killer.

Leslie Nielsen died only recently, at age 84 in 2010. He'll be the victim in "Identity Crisis" (5:3). Later he spoofed police procedurals in the too-brief *Police Squad*.

Richard Anderson went on to "The Six Million Dollar Man," and as of this writing is still alive at 86. Director Norman Lloyd acted with Orson Welles & John Houseman in the Mercury Theater, 75 years ago. He was on "St. Elsewhere" in the 1980s, and at this writing is alive, age 99.

Jessie Royce Landis, playing Susan Clark's mother, Mrs. Chadwick, was Cary Grant's mother in "North By Northwest" and Grace Kelly's mother in "To Catch a Thief." She died three months after the episode first aired.

Susan Clark plays saucy and delish, later playing the prostitute for pubescent pricks in "Porky's."

The Show

Beth Chadwick (Clark) kills her brother Bryce (Anderson) when he bars her consort with Peter Hamilton (Nielsen), the last straw in preventing her from living her own life at all.

Some Quirks include a different start to this one — view of the city from an airplane; doesn't make sense, except Hamilton is coming in that night on a plane. With a phone call from his hotel room, he's not on the plane yet, though. Kinda neat: we see Beth in Bryce's bedroom to swap out keys, and then he's in hers the next day to get shot.

Still too much creepy music for my taste, and still we wonder, *how could the killer have missed that?* She wouldn't see the newspaper, though, and she didn't know Bryce had a spare key. That speech she planned starts to take actual shape — but because it's planned, it's also canned. Oops.

Columbo gets to the house quickly (it's at 2307 Lorraine Drive), the same day as the inquest and having lunch with Hamilton. Is it called an inquest? Because later Beth calls it a "coroner's jury."

There is RED! carpeting and PINK! walls, and Beth Chadwick knows the hairdresser too well — if she's already getting her hair done there, well … she wouldn't have been so mousy, right?

Can you just "assume" the presidency?

Recurring Elements include the third time (out of seven so far) a woman has asked, "You do love me, don't you?" There's the whole thing where you tell the police you're not going to answer any more damn questions — yeah, right. Columbo's careful about money, but manages to take Peter Hamilton to lunch: fast food delivered by waitresses in hot pants, white boots, and stockings … surely a *Quirk*.

In time, Hamilton admits being angry, as "other possible suspects" do when Columbo is clearing them off the list. There's also some business with a cigar, and Columbo seeming clumsy and out of place — as when a woman in the beauty salon almost sprays him with … something. He also pretends not to know things he knows, which allows him to examine the exterior of the house.

Loveable Columbo comes out when dealing with the family: the mother smacks Beth, calls her a child, and says she's incapable of functioning. Columbo recovers control of the situation, says he's impressed with Bryce, and defuses the situation. He faces people down often, without raising his voice. He also is carrying dog treats around all week … though as yet he has no dog.

At one point, Columbo says he and Mrs. Columbo were arguing! It helps him solve the case.

Best Scene

When Beth Chadwick imagines how the murder will go, it shows her plan, and takes proper use of a visual medium, with no clunky explanation. Later, when she shops for a new wardrobe: this shows it's not so much "big changes for the little lady" — but that she was always thus, and now can be. They've done great making her look mousy to this point, and gradually bringing out her nuanced — then pronounced — power: all burgundy velvet, big hat, and enjoying the attention.

Worst Scene

Here I can't decide cleanly whether dialogue where Hamilton begins to break up with Beth is so repetitive from poor writing, or because he's really flustered.

Quotes

"A terrible mistake … mistake … mistake … mistake … mistake … "

"Pretty big place isn't it?"

"I come from a big family. At the dinner table it was like Madison Square Garden."

"Suppose you … "

"I have this bug about tying up loose ends."

"It's gotten her out from under Bryce's thumb."
"Oh yes — way out!"

"I think that in a way, her brother's death is the best thing that ever happened to her."

"You're a police officer?"
"Yes, yes I am."

"Uh, lieutenant? Your cigar."
"What about it?"
"Well, the fragrance is not compatible."

"You look sensational! I'd say you were a new woman."

"Well, what do you think?"
"Interesting."
"What does that mean?"
"It's wild. A little out of your style though, isn't it?"
"No. I don't think it is."

"Well. You asked."
"It was a courtesy. I'm perfectly capable of making my own decisions."

"Am I interrupting something?"
"What do you want, lieutenant?"

"Lieutenant, why are you hounding Beth?"
"Huh? Who me? No, I'm not hounding anybody. Oh no. No, what I'm trying to do is get to the bottom of this thing."

"You don't really think Beth killed her brother in cold blood, now do you?"
"Well, as a matter of fact — I do."

"My wife, she's got a proverb for every situation."

"What do you expect to prove by this bit of nonsense."
"Oh, I'm not trying to prove anything. I came here to arrest you."

"I knew it as soon as I saw that newspaper, but I hadda wait for the proof."

Short Fuse

Episode 1:8

The Players

Killer: Roddy McDowall

Victim: James Gregory

Director: Edward M. Abroms

Writer: Jackson Gillis, Lester Pine, Tina Pine

Columbo appears 20 minutes in; we're more than ¼ done. Roddy McDowall plays the killer; his "Planet of the Apes" co-star Kim Hunter was in "Suitable for Framing" (1:6). His victim Gregory will return for "The Most Crucial Game" (2:3) in a supporting role; he's perhaps best known for "Barney Miller" role as Inspector Frank Luger.

Ida Lupino, McDowall's aunt, will return as a murder victim in the Johnny Cash episode "Swan Song" (3:7). William Windom, Ray Flemming's attorney friend in 1:1 plays an executive VP here. Part of the plan for McDowall is to frame one of the secretaries, Anne Francis, who will be killed in "A Stitch in Crime" (2:6) next season. She died at age 80, in 2011: the same year as Peter Falk.

One of the cops looks a lot like Danny Thomas.

The Show

Roger Stanford finally decides to stop his crazy dazey ways, assuming the presidency of the firm his father started. But he's been such a loser to now that despite (because of?) being a polymath and genius with multiple advanced degrees, his uncle (Gregory) is now plunked right in the way. Moreover Uncle David is selling the company. McDowall's Stanford (note allusion to the school) kills him, and pulls the wool over his Aunt Doris' (Lupino) eyes as well.

Some Quirks include what may be the biggest product placement, since The Brady Bunch went to the Grand Canyon. I mean the Palm Springs Aerial Tramway. Aunt Doris bemoans, "Oh! If he'd only listened to me — if he'd only taken the tram." Meaning he wouldn't have been riding in a car that his nephew planned to blow up. From there, we have several scenes on the tram itself, including several that qualify for *Recurring* and / or *Loveable* entries, as well. Characters even give us data on its construction and operation. Cha-ching!

External shots look like a refinery or other facilities at the massive Port of Los Angeles / Long Beach. In the story they are the company complex, where "Junior," as everyone calls him, has blown $500,000 in research and development (goofing). That's a LOT of money back then.

Others: Uncle David has a photo of himself on his desk … a telephone message system starts to record his voice even though the message saying it will do so continues … Stanford spends the entire day at the apartment of a man he's trying to frame, and the police don't check it out until it's pitch dark

A bankbook!

Who would believe a photographer forgot the negative? In one tram scene, regular people get off — but nobody is waiting in line; so (whew!) we have the next car all to ourselves.

Recurring Elements include a lyin'-ass murderer — who, incidentally (like Dale Kingston), can't stop looking at his watch — as well as a girl he's using. His pride and hubris (every episode ever) manifest in practice jokes and using people.

We also again have more silences — definitely a recurring component at this point. I think I see a typewriter that will return in "Étude in Black" (2:1). Once again, the family of the criminal says "there is no crime" so "you can go now" — this one's version of "no more questions!"

We'll see office renovations in future episodes. Watch at the end for what Stanford does with that national science medal — hanging around his neck the entire show. It's a clever stand in for how the killer often compliments Columbo.

We Love Columbo when he gets scared on the tram ... and then uses it to trap the killer. Did he overcome his fear? Would have been kind of cool to see him at least a little nervous, to maintain that aspect of the lieutenant's personality. He's "not familiar" with Pinewild — the show's stand-in for Idyllwild, where the Buckners have a cabin.

Mrs. Columbo does their taxes.

Best Scene

In the death scene, the music is like a bad outtake from The Monkees, but I still like no talking, this time as the build-up to the explosion: juxtaposition with lightning, a clock, the funky music ... and the boom!

Worst Scene

When Roddy McDowall starts laughing like a hyena at the end. What the HELL is that? There's also the aunt, Doris Buckner, completely agreeing with her nephew at many turns — and quite unconvincingly.

Quotes

"Who are you?"

"The police? You mean that old heap out there is yours?"
"Oh yeah — needs a coat of paint, huh?"

"You might say there's been an excess of corporate bad feeling around here."

"He said he's send over his very best man."
"Is that a fact?"
"Well, my wife, she says I'm second best. But she claims there are 80 fellas tied for first."

"Maybe you better operate this, because I'm not sure how it — "

"Oh these modern idiotic devices. She's not home yet."

"People do look at their watches."
"Yes, they certainly do. Good night."

"They had to use helicopters to build this thing."

"If you step out here on this ledge you'll get a better view."

"Quite by accident, I saw a piece of paper in his wallet."

"We got quite a bit of information from his files. Dossiers actually … "
"Dossiers? What kind of dossiers?"

"Now you've let her see the very thing, I went there to stop her from seeing!"

"Oh, Rog, dear — I've been such a fool."

"Oh Hi Junior! Sorry. Excuse me, Mr. Stanford."

"Lieutenant, would you mind coming to the point?"
"Oh certainly … by the way … "

"They didn't say."
"Seems very peculiar."

"There you go: you're looking at your watch again."

"Will you just shut up!"

"Aren't those supposed to be evidence, Lt. Columbo?"
"Yeah, I guess they are. It's a shame though."

Blueprint for Murder

Episode 1:9

The Players

Killer: Patrick O'Neal

Victim: Forrest Tucker

Director: Peter Falk

Writers: Steven Bochco, William Kelley

Columbo comes in relatively quickly here, at 13 minutes, but with no harm to the story so early, this time. O'Neal and Tucker *command* the screen for the first dozen minutes, communicating scads with verbal asides to secondary characters and slight, back-handed slaps.

O'Neal returns in the last season of the 1970s series for "Make Me A Perfect Murder" (7:3). He's a tough TV executive, a supporting role. He also helped out with two episodes of *McCloud*, one of the other two mystery shows in NBC's original rotation, along with *McMillan and Wife*. So shd it be *McColumbo* … ?

Only directing credit episode of the series for Peter Falk, but IMDB says he worked on "Étude in Black" (2:1), which means that one was an ongoing artistic "discussion" between

Falk, Cassavetes — and maybe Ben Gazzara (d. 2012 at 81) showed up. Cigar buddies and tough-minded actors and directors — and all present in the same room, making a TV show. Awesome to imagine.

Janis Paige, who plays a thoroughly enjoyable first wife of the victim, is 90 as of this writing. And even when Forrest Tucker played someone in the present, he's a cowboy hick.

The Show

Of the four main players, O'Neal's Elliott Markham is the one not named Williamson. Tucker is Bo Williamson, while Janis Paige and Pamela Austin are his first (Goldie) and second (Jennifer) wives. Goldie is the brash and brassy first one who dotes on Columbo; Jennifer is the trophy wife who may be dense: she does not seem to see Markham has marked her out. Tucker *owns* the 10-12 minutes he's on screen.

Their pre-murder conversation more deftly than usual suggests the plan — and reveals it can't look like a murder. The city mouse / country mouse of the musical duel comes into play. When Bo moves to assert his superiority physically, its subdued nature only enhances the act. I credit Falk's direction.

Some Quirks ... Well, knowing what she must know about him, I doubt the secretary wd.

think he'd like "Williamson City." But she perhaps doesn't consider that, in her ardor for her boss and his work. And she plays that very well — defending the executive she "supports" as the EAs say.

So there's no way to get in touch with him in Europe? Where is he? And he lives on "Williamson Ranch" ... but he doesn't want Williamson City? Maybe not at that price. Speaking of which, the units sell for "$30,000 to $36,000 ... apiece." That's meant to be high. It's an interesting concept: be cool to know architectural background for the "cocoon" — sounds ahead of its time; was it?

At one point, Markham says Bo is "flying under a different name" ... ha! Not no more! He slips in suggesting Goldie wants Bo dead to get her 25% of the estate, instead of just alimony: that's dumb because she likes Bo, she'd get both the alimony and the 25% (later) if he stays alive, and that quarter of his estate will no doubt be worth more by then.

Why does he need the dog tags? Surely the heart doctor he's just seen knows Bo's blood type. He could go back and ask him. And the body's in the equipment shed, as if no one goes in there.

Recurring Elements include Forrest Tucker driving in the opening scene: similar to — while distinctly diverging from — "Murder by the Book" (1:3) where the driving is … more methodical.

I wonder if the project that is the external setting for much of the episode is on the Universal lot. There is planted evidence as in (1:2) and O'Neal is surprised, but not uncertain; he's working the plan. Who could be planting evidence, he wonders, and in the shrubbery, no less.

There's a foreshadowing joke about entombing architects and engineers; the claim as in "Dead Weight" (1:5) that something is "pure coincidence;" and Markham's comment that one action is "an exercise in futility." A later episode, "An Exercise in Fatality" (4:1) puns on that. There is the "Suppose we … " staple of veiled threats … again.

Loveable Columbo must spend an entire day in the bureaucratic bowels of L.A. He gets their marriage license (at least 30 years old) and goes back to get blueprints. The segment in lines … almost as good as the Tucker / O'Neal battle but too cliché too win the prize this time. Still great: nobody at information desk … silent soundtrack … told to wait in line … and he needs approval from the Mayor's office. The paperwork jungle is incredible.

When Columbo listens to the country music … yes, it's to reveal the *radio* was on classical; but it's still great to see him sitting there studying it. It's one of those "he's a doofus moments," too.

Overall, Columbo seems more subdued, quieter — even a bit angry, like the first two episodes. He misses his cigar after going to see the heart specialist about Bo (John Fiedler, recognizable soon from his "The Bob Newhart Show" role). In the final scene, as the credits roll, Columbo's about to light up. So he doesn't ... but he still misses them. We know he does.

Best Scene

The scenes between Bo and Markham show the difference between the two men — their musical tastes end up being just a hint of it. Williamson is breaking things, driving maniacally; Markham wants everyone to stop shouting. Markham calls him a Philistine, and Williamson's never heard the word. Honorable mention to the scenes between Columbo and Goldie; she plays it to the gilt ... hilt. She looks like the shiniest member in the Court of the French Sun King.

Worst Scene

Was hard to find a bad one in this episode ... I guess when O'Neal gets the flat, and he lies to the cop, and the cop buys it. Not sure why the scene; tension? So he's thrashed from

changing a tire, *and* he gets caught tonight?
And there's no security at the job site at night,
either.

Quotes

"I don't believe you, ma'am."

"Boy that guy sure is in a hurry."
"Yes. Yes he is."

"I saw him 5 minutes ago when he came in …
Bo! I didn't know you were here!"

"Thanks Miss Sherman. Think I love you."

"These units will be for sale, for all those who
qualify."

"To be absent is not necessarily to be missing,
lieutenant. I assume you know the distinction."

"Did you build this?"
"No, one of my staff did that."

"I call her the 'next-ex' — Oh don't worry
lover: she's half my age and twice as pretty,
but I like her."

"If gold lamé was legal tender I'd rule the
world."

"I dunno what she said but it sounded like she
liked me."

"My friends call me Goldie, and since I'm
standing here nearly naked, we'd better be
friends."

"Oh, then Mr. Markham saw him that day before he left town."

"Are you a policeman?"
"Uh, yes ma'am."

"Is this where he works?"
"Yes, it is."
"Just wonderful."
"Yes, it is."
"Marvelous office."
"Yes, it is."
"Spacious."
"Yes, it is."
"Conference room?"
"Yes, it is."
"Very handy."
"Yes, it is."

"Why do I have the feeling you already know the answer to that question?"

"You want a half a candy bar?"

"Whoever was driving that car musta been listening to classical music. It's confusing."

"Tell me the truth: are you interested in buildings — or in builders?"

"The omnipresent constable."

"The lieutenant was looking for you, Mr. Markham."
"I'm sure he was."

"Quite a lawyer your brother-in-law."
"Yeah I know. The whole family, we're real proud of him."

"See, I figure I gotta come up with something concrete."

"Do you know how much that would cost?"
"No, how much?"

"You just stand there while I give you a kiss. I'm going to love all over you."

"We could've used you at the Alamo. You've got guts."

"I kinda had a hunch."

"Carnegie Hall and Nashville: they don't mix."
"No. No they don't."

Best and Worst Episodes
Season One

Best: Blueprint for Murder

The best episode of Season One is the last one. They have hit their stride and really gotten inside their man, and ours.

In fact, it was hard to find a "worst scene" for the write-up on that episode. And there were too many great scenes — between criminal and victim, between first wife and Columbo, between lieutenant and the bureaucracy that is part of the order he serves.

Directed by Falk, it should be a fan favorite.

Honorable mention to the first two — "Prescription Murder" and "Ransom for a Dead Man" — edgier in lieutenant and tougher in tone, they stand out. Of course, "Murder by the Book" is an episode about writers, directed by Steven Spielberg ... and "Death Lends a Hand" offers Robert Culp ... and "Dead Weight" shows off the OC ...

Worst: Short Fuse

The reason is partly Roddy McDowall, partly the tram, and partly some lousy scenes.

McDowall camps it up too much — it's not overacting, exactly; but it feels like he's thinking, "Well it's TV and it's all just good fun so let's go crazy!" Especially in that last scene … yeesh.

Meanwhile the tram should've gotten credit in the cast for as many scenes as it was in; yes it shows off some beautiful scenery but product placement and too many plot holes (such as a lieutenant who is afraid of heights, then isn't) do it in.

Some of the scenes fall right out of the story, by which I mean they clink out loud and remind us we're watching. Cops checking out an empty apartment at night … characters unbelievable … so we're suddenly aware it's all a sham.

Dishonorable mention "Suitable for Framing" for bush-league mistakes by the criminal and that execrable 15 minutes of falling-to-pieces infamy for Dale Kingston, at the end.

Just One More Thing

Death penalty as luxury tax

Mysteries are for righting not just wrongs but (ultimately) the world. It's just one (more) thing and it's not going to change much. But as they say about the starfish, at least it will change life for *that* one.

Columbo was always about making sure the wealthy didn't get away with it. But money isn't the only problem. It's also hubris and arrogance and even a little stupidity, not to mention cupidity, or, when in its deadly sin form, *greed.*

In the course of righting the wrongs one at a time, mysteries do not actually hide their clues from us. One of the points of a mystery's conclusion is that we could have seen it too and would have, *had we but paid attention* like the detective did.

Columbo amped this up by 1) showing the murder first, and 2) showing the evidence. The first has been much remarked upon; the second is important too, especially as it relates to the cash.

Because what happens in these episodes is we see the effect money has — not just "can have" but ones it actually *does* have, not only in the vast majority of cases, but in all cases, absent our diligence. Of course we always think it'll

be different with us, that we can handle it —
and we joke we'd at least like to try.

I think one thing Columbo says is that even
that isn't such a good plan. Better than
nothing, but still there be dragons along that
route.

For instance, the murder *victims* are usually
wealthy too. So they're filthy rich and stinkers
as a result … but not always. Why do *they* get
the "death penalty" by being killed?

Well it's the *really* evil rich dude (or dudette)
who murders, we say. They're ones who
deserve it. So plausible — maybe counter-
cultural, considering California's death
penalty was invalidated the year after
Columbo began.

Who is Lieutenant Columbo

It seems the most important element of the
show is not the justice meted out to the guilty
— though that *is* vital. It's watching
Lieutenant Columbo, and *how* he goes about
it: the *noticing*, the *asking*, and his (mostly)
guilelessness infusing the entire process.

Watching these episodes again and again (and
again) for this book gave me a new
appreciation for this. It showed me the care
taken with the work itself, and the building of
just who Columbo is: soft-spoken, direct,

honest, earnest … and, of course, afraid of heights.

The more we pay attention (in this case to Columbo himself) the more we're in on all this: the work of the show, and the actions of the man. We know it's there, but now we see its importance — just a bit more.

And even when the facts sometimes get mixed up over time, the truth remains.